A Special Gift

FOR:

....

FROM:

....

DATE:

....

DEDICATED TO MY SOUL MATE, TO SOUL SEEKERS,
AND ALL THE LOST SOULS IN THE WORLD
LOOKING TO FIND THEIR WAY.

Illustration Copyright © 2001

Text Copyright © 2001
The Brownlow Corporation
6309 Airport Freeway
Fort Worth, Texas 76117

ISBN: 1-57051-969-2

Printed in China

SEVENTY-FIVE WAYS TO

Calm Your Soul

by JULIE GRANGER

Brownlow

Little Treasures Miniature Books

To have strong roots is perhaps what the human soul needs most though we may not know it.

UNKNOWN

1. Listen to the music of silence,
the symphony of water, and the gentle strum
of your heart strings as you calm your soul.

2. Be prepared. Plan for the next day and make
a list. It will help make your day go smoother.

3. Find a serene place to relax in order
to develop your spiritual grace.

4. Begin everyday with the Lord
to renew your spirit.
Reconnect and start anew.

5. Avoid negative people for they drain your
energy and deplete your soul.

6. Sit long enough to listen to what the Lord
is trying to tell you.

7. Discover who your true friends are for
they will strengthen your soul.

8. Lay a good foundation to weather the
storms of life. Friends and family can
provide strong anchors when the winds of
change blow through our lives.

No gift is too small to give

nor too simple to receive,

If it is chosen with

thoughtfulness

and given with love.

UNKNOWN

9. Visit a museum for an afternoon and absorb the visual messages. Search for the painting that speaks to you.

10. Take a nap to calm your soul. No day is so bad that it can not be fixed with a nap.

11. Choose a new goal for the week or the month. Reward yourself when you accomplish it.

12. Receive the gifts that God has given to you. Use them for the greater good.

13. Accept praise with grace and offer
compliments with sincerity.

14. Remember the books that you read,
the people that you spend time with, and the
lifestyle that you lead affect your soul.

15. Walk through a forest or a garden and
stop to rest. Feel the energy of life
and the power of nature.

16. Nurture the expressive side of
your soul. Dance, paint, and sing
as if no one is watching.

The light of God
surrounds me,
the love of God enfolds me,
the power of God protects me,
the presence of God
watches over me.
Wherever I am God is.

PRAYER CARD

17. Create a special haven of peace
to rest and dream and plan and think.

18. Look out a window and relax;
breathe deep and straighten out the day.

19. Surround your life with quotes that inspire
and give your mind food for thought.

20. Help others to find
the same joy you
have discovered in your soul.

21. Enjoy the company of others and appreciate the moment.

22. Write down what you think, and it will help you discover the pathways to your soul.

23. Take a bubble bath and surround yourself with serenity.

24. Cleanse the soul of past pain, hurt, regret, remorse, and guilt. God will be there, just as a rainbow appears after the rain.

Never lose an opportunity of seeing anything that is beautiful; for beauty is God's handwriting — a wayside sacrament.

RALPH WALDO EMERSON

25. Meditate to welcome the morning.

26. To be lost in our soul is painful and lonely. Reconnect with your inner spirit and recapture the joy one step at a time.

27. Learn to pat yourself on the back and praise your attributes right out loud.

28. Open your heart to animals, and be prepared to receive unconditional love in return.

29. Learn to make decisions and stand behind them.

30. Dance, move, breathe, and stretch
beyond your wildest dreams.

31. Have faith in the Lord and believe that
with your prayers and his guidance,
things will work out for the good.

32. Concentrate on things that are noble and
make spiritually wise choices.

33. Hold hands when you need to
on your journey through life.

A heart

at peace

gives life to

the body.

PROVERBS 14:30

34. Gain perspective by looking at things
from a different point of view.

35. Search for the books that speak to your soul;
the ones that will make a difference in
your life. There are books
out there waiting for you.

36. Sit on a park bench and
feed the birds. Soak up the shade
or bask in the sunlight.
Relax and enjoy the moment.

37. Look for guidance to renew your soul
and ask for help when you need it.

38. Write letters to old friends.
Let them know how much they mean to you.

39. Reveal your soul though your actions.
Participate in this adventure called life.

40. Listen to soothing music to restore
balance in your life.

O Lord, support us all day long, until the shadows lengthen, and the evening comes, the busy world is hushed, and the fever of the day is over.

JOHN HENRY CARDINAL NEWMAN

41. Honor the beauty inside and nurture the true meaning of what is important.

42. Apply wisdom to daily living. It will have a profound effect on your inner life and your relationships with others.

43. Share your strengths with the world and receive gifts of love in return.

44. Release your worries to God through prayer.

45. Stop, catch your breath,
and be thankful.

46. Be tolerant of your weaknesses and
proud of your strengths.

47. Allow yourself a mental health day
and spend time caring for your soul.
Give yourself permission to
take time for yourself.

Bless the Lord,

O my soul;

and all that is within me,

bless His holy name.

PSALM 103:1

48. Find in your heart what you believe
and follow it.

49. Take care of yourself so you
will be there when others need you.

50. Love yourself and
others unconditionally.

51. Drink a cup of hot tea or hot
chocolate and allow the warmth
to simmer deep inside.

52. Take time to walk into beautiful old shops that have antique books scattered amongst baskets of yarn with wind chimes hanging near a window and soft music playing in the background.

53. Believe with all of your heart and soul that with God's help you can do anything.

54. Give, share, and forgive without strings attached. Make a difference in the lives of others.

God has put

something noble and good

into every heart.

His hand created.

MARK TWAIN

55. Make a list of all your frustrations.
Get them out of your system and let them go.

56. Let words of kindness rain down
on you like a plant that needs nourishment.
Daily doses of positive reassurance
can help your soul to blossom.

57. Do what you love and follow your heart.
Plant seeds of love and harvest
rewards of joy.

58. Weed out the negative chatter that races through your mind. This barrage of negative conversations can erode your very core and cloud your thoughts.

59. Share your time with the ones you care about most.

60. Remember the Lord has prepared and guided you to this time in your life. How you use your time is up to you.

My songs rise to God,

as an eagle to the sun.

VICTOR HUGO

Be still and know

that I am God.

PSALM 46:10

61. Dare to reach inside and discover
all your God-given potential.
The power and knowledge will give your
spirit wings to soar to new heights.

62. Take a chance. Take the first step
to discover what life has to offer.

63. Watch fish glide through the water
and butterflies flutter in the air.

64. Count your blessings
and write them down.

65. Yell at somebody on paper, then throw it away. Choose not to carry anger around with you.

66. Have a daily conversation with the Lord and don't forget to say thank you.

67. Take inventory of the positive aspects in your life. Remember the Lord has given you everything you need to be happy.

68. Overcome an old fear and experience the new freedom it has to offer.

Thinking is the talking of the soul with itself.

PLATO

God is our refuge and strength, a very present help in trouble.

PSALM 46:1

69. Take some small step every day to move closer to your dreams. You have the power within to make your dreams come true.

70. Praise the Giver. Celebrate human life for it is a gift from God.

71. Indulge your sweet tooth with decadent ice cream bars loaded with chocolate, caramel, and nuts. Everyone deserves a treat now and then.

72. Make a list of the people you have hurt and ask for forgiveness. Start with yourself.

73. Define your dream and write it down
to see what it looks like.
Then tell someone you trust.

74. Give those you love the gifts
of undivided attention, unending
enthusiasm, and creative energy.

75. Exchange negative attitudes with
positive ones. Replacing anger with
compassion, arrogance with humility,
and stress with serenity can bring
peace to any situation.

Ask, and it shall be given to you; seek and you shall find; knock, and it shall be opened unto you.

MATTHEW 7:7

I believe that life is given to us

so that we may grow in love and I

believe that God is in me as the sun is

in the color and fragrance of a flower.

HELEN KELLER